VILLAGE TO VILLAGE (V2V)

Joseph E James

Outpouring Press

CONTENTS

Village To Village (V2V)©
is an Evangelistic Discipleship Initiative of
Higher Ground Ministries

PROLOGUE

We were going from Village to Village in a farming region in central Kenya. We came to a farm and saw a woman sat on a chair in front of one of her fields. She did not speak any English, so as our team talked to her, I walked with her husband and the pastor to look at their goats. We walked back to where his wife was sitting and one of the women, the pastor's wife, Cadence, told me what the lady had told her. She had badly broken her shin a year earlier. When the bone healed it left her unable to walk far. She had been a hard-working farmer and was no longer able to work her fields. Due to the stress of this she was depressed. She could not feel her leg from the knee down.

I instructed Cadence to ask the farmer if she could lay her hand on her leg and pray for her. I then instructed her how to pray for the farmer. While she was doing this I was explaining to the rest of the team what was happening. I could see that the farmer's leg was not healing. I had Cadence ask the farmer if there was any difference. There was not. She prayed again. I started talking to the Holy Spirit inwardly, and discerned that there was a demon, a spirit of fear. In the Spirit I could see this serpent like figure coiled around her leg. Its tail by the woman's ankle, and the head by her knee. When Cadence had finished praying for her, she looked a little sad because nothing was happening. I told Cadence what the Lord had shown me.

Doing this stuff is fun, and there is room for laughter and joy to be present, we're bringing "Good News". With that in my mind I smiled and said, "Okay, reach out like you're grabbing the snake by the tail, and pull it off her leg. Say 'Spirit of fear leave in Jesus' name!'" What happened next is priceless. Cadence, who had never seen a person healed that she had prayed for, nor seen a demon leave when she prayed, yanked that demon off that farmer's leg. Immediately the farmer started reaching for her leg with wide open eyes, saying something like "Oh, Oh, Oh, Oh!" she started talking in her dialect and I asked, excitedly, "What's happening, what is she saying?". All feeling was returning to her leg and it was so sudden it shocked her. Cadence's face was a picture too, eyes as wide as her open mouth. I said "Okay Cadence, take her for a walk down to the goats and back. Speak healing over her in Jesus' name and she will be fine".

The next day we were up at the church building and these two women walked up to say hello. One of them was the farmer. She had walked three miles to come and show us what Jesus had done for her. Completely healed!

Where Did This Book Come From?

Initially this piece of work was compiled as a training manual. It was time to put on paper the things that I was taught, and the things that I have learned over the thirty years that I have been doing this stuff. Back in my home country of Wales, I was fortunate to grow up in a church with a pastor who was an evangelist. We were trained up to the gills in anything evangelism orientated. For example, I learned how to do Mime in order to present the Gospel through that medium. It took me into prisons, schools, festivals, churches, on the streets, preaching the Gospel without saying a word. Ray Boltz's "Watch the Lamb" was always a winner. I often cried as I performed the choreography I learned from my teacher. I also played piano as part of a worship team; we belted out the Gospel through music. We knocked thousands of doors, distributed thousands more flyers, prayed for the sick, led many to Christ. This is what we did. We rubbed shoulders with leaders who were advancing the Gospel across the nations. In fact, our group of churches had preached the Gospel in all 195 nations recognized by the UN. I am grateful for those good influences.

I moved to America in 2007. In 2008 I joined a church of about seventy people, and by 2010 it had grown to over seven hundred people. From 2009 to 2010, I had the privilege of teaching on the Kingdom of God in that church, at a bi-weekly class. We saw many healings and miracles. Then I was asked by another ministry to be an associate pastor in a new church plant. This ministry did a lot of work with the poor, and the homeless of St Louis. They also had a Healing Rooms. It was great to be exposed to many new experiences.

That same year, through one of the Houses of Prayer in the city, I met a man who became a friend. He had been an intern with Randy Clark, and Global Awakening. Suddenly I was introduced to Deliverance Ministry. I had always been turned off by the examples I had seen of scared people cowering, as the preacher yelled at the demons. It always seemed wrong to me. I had no experience with that kind of ministry. But now I was seeing something completely different, and it worked too. None of the drama, just the power of Jesus setting people free. I wanted to learn more. My friend taught me, and in 2012 I went to India for the first time, and man it kicked off. I'm still processing what the Lord did there. I saw my first real deliverance, and then many strange experiences where darkness was pushed back by the power of the Gospel. I knew that this was something that others needed to learn.

We need more powerful experiences in the Church. Not hype, but simple, pure, moves of the Holy Spirit as He manifests the will of Jesus in our cities. We are living in days, in some regions, that are akin to the pre-gospel days of the Bible. In other areas, we are seeing post-Christian days. This is where my desire to produce a manual comes from. To equip believers to move in the power of the Gospel. When you read about the early church, you see men and women moving in power. Jesus showed them, and then said "Repeat this!". That's the expectation.

Dotted i's, Crossed t's

I would like to thank Josh Clark for giving me permission to add Randy Clark's teaching on the Five Step Healing Model, and the Ten Step Deliverance Model. I have researched and looked at many different models, and keep coming back to these two models. I love how pastoral they are, and how powerful they are. They work! They prioritize the person being prayed for, and not some show and dance with egos and demons. So, thank you Global Awakening for these notes. As we have done missions in other countries, they have been generous in donating their "Prayer Cards" that support these models. I have provided the details of how to obtain these "Prayer Cards" from Global Awakening's store in the Healing and Deliverance section of this book. Please do yourself a favor and purchase your own copy from them. Those "Prayer Cards" are gold.

Concerning the language and format of the book, I chose to write it as though I have a classroom of people in front of me. I refer to "our team", and they consist of those, past and present, who use this book to train teams.

I also have some sentences in bold lettering for emphasis. That is more of a training manual format, than a book. I just feel those points are key points.

My heart is for you to train others. As you become proficient, then you can teach others. Where I have put my own personal stories, in order to teach a point, you can replace them with your own stories, as you train others. This will add authenticity to your teaching, and also spread the word of the wonderful things God does.

This finally brings me to the title. Well, it's out of the Bible:

"They set out and went from <u>village to village</u>, proclaiming
the good news and healing people everywhere"
(Luke 9:6)

I did add the "V2V" just as a catchy acronym, similar to those used by many other ministries. I do hope to expand and add to this work over the years. There is more to teach on other areas pertaining to evangelism and Church planting. For now, my prayer is that you blaze in the power of the Holy Spirit, and go from Village To Village igniting the world on fire with love for Jesus!

Joseph E James, 2022

FOREWORD BY AUTHOR

Welcome to our Village To Village (V2V)© discipleship course. You are about to embark on a journey of making famous the name of Jesus from Village to Village, Town to Town, City to City, and Nation to Nation. We are going to teach you how to use the tools that Jesus has given His disciples for reaching the lost, and also principles for helping new Believers walk their new life with Jesus.

Here are some priorities that we value:

- People – We want to LOVE people the way Jesus does. We want to show love in ways that people feel it. To the hungry it is food. To the lonely it is comfort and friendship. To the sick it is healing. To the demonized it is deliverance, and to the lost it is Salvation.

- Effectiveness – We aim to be an effective ministry. What we mean by this is that the lost find Jesus, the sick walk away healed, and those tormented by demons walk away free.

- YOU! – Contained within these notes, and in the lives of your teachers, are decades and decades of experience of serving through evangelism, miracles, signs, wonders, church planting, preaching and many other areas. We are here to help, not to hinder. You are not just another person; you are an answer to someone's prayer. You are a walking miracle. You are a vessel of honor in the Hands of God as He sends you in the Power of the Holy Spirit to introduce Jesus to people who need to meet Him.

• A Powerful Framework – The reason why we are going to teach you various models for healing, deliverance, and preaching the Gospel, is to give us all a framework to operate within. We are aware that you all come from different backgrounds and experiences, we want to honor that. However, just like a Soccer team, there are different players with different skills, but they all train together and work to a common gameplan. Consider these reasons why:

1) To protect the people we minister to - We must be loving and reassuring to those we are ministering to. Sometimes it can be scary for a person when a demon is leaving their body. We must not add to the tension of the moment with strange ministry styles.

2) "But all things should be done decently and in order" (1 Cor. 14:40*) - By following the structures that we will teach you then we know that wherever you go you will conduct yourselves with order and dignity. To some of you these teachings and experiences will be new - We are helping you to develop into an effective minister of the Gospel. When I was learning the "Deliverance Model" I would ask myself constantly "What was I taught to do?", but now I am in a place where I have learned what to do. You too will find your own voice, and way of ministering.

• God's Glory – Jesus said "By this my Father is glorified,

that you bear much fruit and so prove to be my disciples" (John 15:8) - we do not want to draw attention to ourselves or our ministry, but rather it is all for the Glory of God. You will develop a greater love for people. In this way you will care for people when no one is looking, when you don't have an audience. You will love and pray for a person when you do not feel any power, or you think the "anointing" has lifted. You will keep praying, pressing through, and showing love to them. When we live for His Glory then He is all the audience we need.

*All Scripture references will be from the English Standard Version unless otherwise stated.

INTRODUCTION
DYNAMIC DISCIPLES
& APPRENTICES OF
ACTION

C an you imagine having a teacher like Jesus? I wonder what it felt like, back then, to be called by Him to be one of his disciples. In the Bible language a word that more accurately describes a "disciple" is the word "apprentice". Here is a definition of an "apprentice":

> "A person who works for an employer for a fixed period of time in order to learn the particular skills needed in their job"
> (Oxford Dictionary)

I would like to explain what we mean by "apprentice", and what we don't mean.

Our aim, as trainers, is to disciple you in the ways of ministry according to Jesus' lifestyle and teaching. Even though we will be using certain models of ministry (for healing, deliverance, and sharing the Gospel), we use them to set you on the right course toward effective ministry. Simply put, these models work! But as you will see, and learn, it is the Holy Spirit that we will follow. The models are mere protocols, frameworks in which to minister, to protect you and others, but the Holy Spirit can add to them and lead us away from them.

These models are like when we learned how to walk as children. We would use a table, a chair, or even our mother's leg to help us balance. But once we learned how to walk, we no longer needed those things. So too will these models help you find your feet, and walk confidently when ministering to people.

True discipleship, and apprenticeship, is to train people to have their own walk with Jesus. We are not into cloning, or mass production of the same product. Our aim is to teach you how to walk with Jesus, as yourself, in a deeper and more powerful way.

Paul said:

"Follow my example, as I follow the example of Christ"
(1 Corinthians 11:1 NIV)

Other translations say:

"Be imitators of me, as I am of Christ"

He is encouraging his followers to follow his example of following Christ. The aim is to follow Jesus, not Paul. Otherwise, I will relate to Christ as Paul, and not as myself! We're not saying that we can't learn from a "Paul".

We're saying that the immediate goal is to disciple believers to walk with Christ, this in turn means, like Paul, I can show you what that looks like, because I too walk with Jesus.

He, Jesus, will develop in you Christ-likeness. We're not after Paul-likeness, **we want Christ-likeness** (John 10:27, 2 Corinthians 3:18, Romans 8:5-9, Philippians 2:5, 1 Peter 2:21-23).

You are disciples and apprentices of Jesus, first!

A leader should disciple you to have your own walk with Christ. A leader should not be intimidated by the closeness of your walk with Jesus, or the power of your gifting and calling. They will understand how much of a blessing you will be to them, and not a threat, because of your walk with Jesus. A secure leader will free you to follow the call of God on your life. Spiritual maturity, then, is attained, and developed, by living your life for Jesus, by His wisdom and guidance, through the power of the Holy Spirit, to the Glory of God (John 15:8). Our aim is to better help you accomplish that.

John wrote:

"But the anointing that you received from him abides in you, and you have no need that anyone should teach you. But as his anointing teaches you about everything, and is true, and is no lie —just as it has taught you, abide in him"
(1 John 2:27)

Let me clarify this amazing verse without changing what it says. For example, if I do not know how to fly a plane then I will need a lot of instruction, so it does not mean that man cannot teach us anything. However, the Holy Spirit could teach you how to fly a plane, supernaturally. The main thing is just don't get weird when it comes to these things. Also, don't go trying to fly a plane to prove me wrong! We need Teachers, otherwise Jesus would not have given them to the Church (Ephesians 4:11-12). For me, 1 John 2:27 is the fulfillment of true discipleship and apprenticeship.

Paul, writing to Galatia, said:

"For I did not receive it from any man, nor was I taught it, but I received it through a revelation of Jesus Christ"
(Galatians 1:12)

I trust that you can see that we are not going to clone ourselves, or mass produce ourselves, but rather train you in **the works of**

Christ, so that you can walk with Christ, like Christ, in the power of Christ! Also, it needs to be said – Many, if not all of you, already have amazingly powerful walks with Christ! We will learn from each other how to do it better, as Paul said:

> "For I long to see you, that I may impart to you some spiritual gift to strengthen you—that is, <u>that we may be mutually encouraged by each other's faith</u>, both yours and mine"
> (Romans 1:11-12)

At the end of the day that's what we care about - walking with Him, and effectively representing Him. **How can we represent Him if we do not know Him? How can we know Him if we do not walk with Him?**

CHAPTER 1
IT MUST BE LOVE,
LOVE, LOVE!

L et us look at the number one heart-position of a true apprentice of Jesus.

Paul said:

> "If I speak in the tongues of men and of angels, but have
> not love, I am a noisy gong or a clanging cymbal. And if I
> have prophetic powers, and understand all mysteries and all
> knowledge, and if I have all faith, so as to remove mountains, but
> have not love, I am nothing"
> (1 Corinthians 13:1-2)

The undergirding perfect element in all of what we do is LOVE! That is why being an apprentice of Jesus is not just about moving in signs and wonders. I've seen countless ministers networking to build their Empires, they are ambitious. I've seen others do ministry to feel wanted or appreciated. I've even seen those who do ministry in order to prove somebody else wrong. These are all poor motivators. **There must be something deeper**

that motivates us than ambition, or a need to feel wanted, or even a vendetta. <u>**LOVE is the right motivation!**</u> Love is the greatest motivation because it is pure and unsullied by ulterior impulses. **Love for Him and love for people** - *"For Christ's love compels us"* **(2 Corinthians 5:14a NIV)**.

One preacher said it like this:

> "Love, morally, is the desire to benefit others, even at the expense of self, because love desires to give"
> Ed Cole

This is the cure to our selfishness. If you are thinking *"How will ministry benefit ME. What will I get for doing this?"*, then maybe "Ministry" is not the right thing for you. The word "Ministry" means "to serve".

Jesus said it best:

> "The Son of Man came not to be served but to serve"
> (Matthew 20:28)

That's our glorious example. When "Ministry" is about ME, then it ceases to be about HIM, and it ceases to be true ministry. We are pouring ourselves out for those He sends us to.

As apprentices we are learning the skills needed for the task ahead. It would be terrible if you trained under a carpenter for three years, and after those three years you could not saw wood in half, or use a hammer properly. Just imagine training to be a farmer and after your apprenticeship is over you still do not know how to feed and care for cows, sheep, goats, or how to plough a field, or even how to plant seed. You would not succeed as a farmer; you would suffer ruin.

<u>**Jesus wants His apprentices to be well trained, well informed, and productive.**</u> He knows that as you learn His ways you will grow. He even said:

> "Take my yoke upon you, and learn from me, for I am gentle

and lowly in heart, and you will find rest for your souls"
(Matthew 11:29)

He wants us to learn!

If the first lesson is LOVE! What's next? This may be open to interpretation, but for me, in light of Jesus' commission to His disciples, it has to do with "Power and Authority", which we will look at in depth later on.

What is the "Gospel"?

In 1953, during the Coronation ceremony of Queen Elizabeth II, a Bible was handed to her and these words spoken to her:

"We present you with this Book, the most valuable thing that this world affords. Here is Wisdom; This is the royal Law; These are the lively Oracles of God"
(Gideons Bible Introduction)

The heart of God issues forth a love letter. A Divine telegram in human form – Jesus. Even though Jesus walked freely among man, we must remember that he took on the form of man (Philippians 2:5-8). The Messenger, and the Message, remained Divine. The Gospel is not a Philosophy. Philosophy is the love of knowledge. It is the systematic approach of ordering and pondering knowledge. Therefore, the Gospel is never to be brought down to a human level and philosophized. No, from Divinity it came and treated as Divine it must be received, and delivered. For it to be understood requires the auspices of the Holy Spirit as he raises the penitent to a Divine level. For it is not scientific, it is not something that can be observed in a glass jar. Rather it is a realm that we enter and live in, and therefore understand through revelation and experience.

As you will see in this section that the Proclamation and Demonstration of the Gospel is mysterious. It is never a muffled bugle squawk, but a pristine trumpet call (1 Corinthians 14:7-17). It is both subtle and obvious, simple yet sublimely complex. It is to be heard and heeded. When clearly presented it demands a response.

The word "Gospel" (**Gk: euaggélion**) means:

- The good news of the coming of the Messiah (Strong's)

- Literally, "God's good news." The Gospel includes the entire Bible, i.e. it is not limited to how a person becomes a Christian (HELPS Word-Studies)

The Gospel is a power-message, and without demonstrations of power the message is not fully delivered! Or put another way – **The Gospel is a powerful message, and we need to be empowered to fully deliver it!**

Throughout history many missionaries have been sent into the world with, for want of a better word, a "powerless" Gospel. Maybe the denomination, or organized church they belonged to did not believe that miracles happen today. However, God has still used these faithful servants, and I do not want to take away from their great sacrifice as that would be dishonorable. The Gospel they preached was focused on living among people, and through living out Christian values they hoped to inspire the people around them. Many mission groups went with money to build schools and hospitals to extend the good news through education and caring for the sick. These are all admirable efforts, and I believe they are an important part of the Gospel.

Paul said it like this:

"For I will not venture to speak of anything except what Christ has accomplished through me to bring the Gentiles to obedience —by word and deed, by the power of signs and wonders, by the power of the Spirit of God—so that from Jerusalem and all the way around to Illyricum I have fulfilled the ministry of the gospel of Christ"
(Romans 15:18-19)

Look at how the New Living Translation renders this verse:

"Yet I dare not boast about anything except what Christ has done through me, bringing the Gentiles to God <u>by my message and by the way I worked among them. They were convinced by the power of miraculous signs and wonders and by the power of God's Spirit.</u> In this way, <u>I have fully presented the Good News of Christ</u> from Jerusalem all the way to Illyricum"

Can people get saved just by hearing the preaching of the Gospel? Of course! Sometimes that's all we may get opportunity to do. As mentioned, there are sections of the Church who do not believe that the Holy Spirit moves in the Church today like He did in the New Testament. They preach the Gospel, and people are saved, and they do good works i.e. building schools, hospitals, aid, charity etc.

Luke records the words of Peter at Cornelius' house:

"God anointed Jesus of Nazareth with the Holy Spirit and with power. He went about doing good and healing all who were oppressed by the devil, for God was with him"
(Acts 10:38)

That phrase – doing good – means that Jesus did:

· good deeds, (and) performed kind service (Strong's)

Peter is clear to note that this was in addition to "healing all who were oppressed by the devil".

James said:

"One of you says to them, 'Go in peace, be warmed and filled,' without giving them the things needed for the body, what good is that?"
(James 2:16)

Paul also echoes this important part of demonstrating the

Gospel in this way:

> "So then, as we have opportunity, let us do good to everyone, and especially to those who are of the household of faith"
> (Galatians 6:10)

I love Simmons' rendering in The Passion Translation:

> "Take advantage of every opportunity to be a blessing to others, especially to our brothers and sisters in the family of faith!"

In the same way that Peter noted Jesus' good works and healing of the oppressed, I believe that these constituted **clear demonstrations of supernatural events**. I believe that the presence of supernatural events enables us to say that we have fully presented the Gospel. Jesus did everything as One led by His Father in the power of the Holy Spirit. It wasn't only the miracles that were supernatural events, no, equally Him giving money to the poor, or comforting someone who was mourning, or preaching and teaching - they were all supernatural. They flowed from who He was, the perfect representation of the Father (Hebrews 1:3).

There are many unbelievers in this world who show charity, and the world needs that. However, the difference between when an unbeliever shows charity, and when a believer shows charity, is this issue of being an extension of God's love to people. We are empowered, and authorized, to display His love. Where a charity, that raises money for cancer research, can accomplish a lot, the believer is empowered to heal cancer in Jesus' name. With Christ we can do what others can't.

Look again at what Paul said! He specifically references what Christ accomplished through him and concluded that he had fully presented the Gospel, and it was done by:

> "Word and deed, by the power of signs and wonders, by the

power of the Spirit of God"
(Romans 15:18b-19a)

Look even at how Paul concludes his thoughts on this:

"As it is written, 'Those who have never been told of him will
see, and those who have never heard will understand'"
(Romans 15:21)

What a strange thing to say that those *"who have never been
told of him will see"*, usually when you tell somebody something
then they hear what you tell them. I am therefore convinced that
we cannot separate Proclamation and Demonstration, for they are
two sides of the same coin called the "Gospel".

Let's look at some familiar verses in the book of Romans:

"For I am not ashamed of the gospel, for it is the power of God
for salvation to everyone who believes, to the Jew first and also to
the Greek. For in it the righteousness of God is revealed from faith
to faith, as it is written, "The righteous shall live by faith."
(Romans 1:16-17)

Look at verse seventeen, it says:

"For in it the righteousness of God is revealed"

In what? In the Gospel! This is where the righteousness of God
is REVEALED! That word means to:

- uncover, bring to light - (Strong's)
- apokalýptō- uncover, revealing what is hidden (veiled,
  obstructed), especially its inner make-up; to make plain
  (manifest) – (HELPS Word Study)

As you will see when we look at our foundational Scriptures
in the next section, what Paul did through Proclamation and
Demonstration, is what Jesus taught His disciples to do:

"And proclaim as you go, saying, 'The kingdom of heaven is
at hand.' Heal the sick, raise the dead, cleanse lepers, cast out

demons..."
(Matthew 10:7-8a)

Jesus gave them a very short sermon "The kingdom of heaven is at hand". It was one-part Proclamation ("The kingdom of heaven is at hand") and four-parts Demonstration (Heal the sick, raise the dead, cleanse lepers, cast out demons).

Both Jesus' initial commission to His early disciples, all the way to the Gospel entrusted to Paul (Romans 2:16, 2 Timothy 2:8, Titus 1:3), was **Proclamation (preaching and teaching) and Demonstration (signs, wonders, healings, raising the dead, deliverances, good works etc.), this constituted the** *full* **presentation of the Gospel.**

In this way, I propose, that it is through both Proclamation and Demonstration that the "Gospel" is fully delivered.

As a practical illustration, by using the example of Proclamation and Demonstration being different sides of the same coin, please take a coin from your pocket or your purse. On one side of the coin, you may have the head of a notable representative of your country, and on the other side of the coin the monetary value of the coin. **FLIP IT** up in the air! As it flips and rotates you will see both the notable person's head and the monetary value blending as though one image. So too does the Proclamation and Demonstration of the Gospel blend seamlessly to the point where you do not realize that when you are praying for the sick that you are actually preaching. And when you are speaking then you are confirming that *"Those who have never been told of him will see"*. It is a mysteriously great Gospel!

Why is this important?

Again, as mentioned, many times missionaries are part of denominations who do not believe that Jesus still does miracles today. Therefore, they have no appetite, or expectation, for supernatural things. John G Lake, who planted 700 churches in five years (1908-1913), in South Africa, wrote in one of his letters to a friend:

"Missionaries without faith for healing do not amount to much in this country"
John G Lake

This is a real problem in countries who have Witch Doctors, Black Priests, and those who move in the same demonic powers as Pharoah's magicians. Lake saw that Christians cannot compete with these powers if they did not move in the greater power of Jesus. Therefore, with intentionality, and by faith, we must be aware of the Holy Spirit's presence with us to powerfully manifest this great message that has been entrusted to us.

For the sake of balance:

On the other side of the story, even today, many preachers have blown into a city with mass Gospel festivals. They note how many make decisions for Christ, how many miracles are performed, and they take their photos and then they essentially, leave! *I generalize for the sake of this following point* - I have had many Pastors from third world countries say to me that while they appreciate that the ministers come, and with much money put on big events; ultimately, they are left sad. Why? because after these festivals the people of their nation go home hungry, uneducated, and poor. Even though the people saw the power of the Gospel through preaching, miracles, healings etc. it did not change their lives in ways that broke the cycle of poverty.

This is where I feel our vision for Village To Village (V2V)©, and the work of Higher Ground Ministries, will join the two forms of evangelism. It is inspired by that beautiful verse in the Gospel of Luke, whereby Jesus had empowered and sent His apprentices out:

> "They set out and went from village to village,
> proclaiming the good news and healing people everywhere"
> (Luke 9:6 NIV)

It's that simple!

As the Lord sends us out, **we will go from Village to Village (town, city) and preach the Good News and heal people everywhere (Spirit, Soul, and Body - 1 Thessalonians 5:23)!** Not "meeting to meeting", but Village to Village. We will see where the Lord is moving significantly and then we will plant a Church in that village, town, or city, as the Lord leads. That place will become a base for evangelizing that area, and **we will train up those who have come to Jesus to go out and do what we did to introduce them to Jesus. Village to Village!**

However, we are looking at a bigger picture too. We aim to, by the grace of God, break the cycle of poverty through education, business/employment opportunities and whatever else is needed to raise a village up as a beacon to the favor and Glory of God (Proverbs 11:11).

This is why we are very excited that you are with us today to join us on this journey.

CHAPTER 2
FOUNDATIONAL
SCRIPTURES

J esus was very specific when sending the twelve disciples, the
seventy-two other disciples, then all believers. In the verses
that follow we can see His wisdom and commissioning.

Sending the Twelve:

"And he called to him his twelve disciples and <u>gave them
authority over unclean spirits, to cast them out, and to heal
every disease and every affliction</u>…These twelve <u>Jesus sent out</u>,
instructing them, "Go nowhere among the Gentiles and enter
no town of the Samaritans, but go rather to the lost sheep of the
house of Israel. And proclaim as you go, saying, '<u>The kingdom of
heaven is at hand. Heal the sick, raise the dead, cleanse lepers, cast
out demons.</u> You received without paying; give without pay"
(Matthew 10:1, 5-8)

"And he went up on the mountain and called to him those
whom he desired, and they came to him. And he appointed twelve
(whom he also named apostles) so that they might be with him
and he might <u>send them out to preach</u> and <u>have authority to cast
out demons</u>"
(Mark 3:13-15)

"And he called the twelve and began to <u>send them out two by two</u>, and <u>gave them authority over the unclean spirits</u>...So they went out and proclaimed <u>that people should repent</u>. And <u>they cast out many demons and anointed with oil many who were sick and healed them</u>"
(Mark 6:7, 12)

"And he called the twelve together and <u>gave them power and authority</u> over <u>all demons</u> and to <u>cure diseases</u>, and he sent them out <u>to proclaim the kingdom of God and to heal</u>...And they departed and went from village to village, <u>preaching the gospel and</u>
<u>healing people everywhere</u>"
(Luke 9:1-2, 6)

Sending the Seventy-Two:

"After this the Lord appointed seventy-two others and <u>sent them</u> on ahead of him, two by two, into every town and place where he himself was about to go...Whenever you enter a town... <u>Heal the sick in it and say</u> to them, '<u>The kingdom of God has come near to you</u>'...The seventy-two returned with joy, saying, "Lord, even <u>the demons are subject to us in your name!</u>" And he said to them, 'I saw Satan fall like lightning from heaven. Behold, <u>I have given you authority to tread on serpents and scorpions, and over all the power of the enemy, and nothing shall hurt you</u>. Nevertheless, do not rejoice in this, that the spirits are subject to you, but rejoice that your names are written in heaven'"
(Luke 10:1, 8-9, 17-20)

Other Commissions:

"And Jesus came and said to them, '<u>All authority in heaven and on earth</u> has been given to me. <u>Go therefore and make disciples of all nations</u>, baptizing them in the name of the Father and of the

Son and of the Holy Spirit, teaching them to observe all that I have commanded you. And behold, I am with you always, to the end of the age'"
(Matthew 28:18-20)

"And behold, I am sending the promise of My Father upon you. But <u>remain in the city until you have been clothed with power from on high</u>"
(Luke 24:49)

"Jesus said to them, 'Peace be with you. <u>As the Father has sent Me, so also I am sending you</u>' When He had said this, <u>He breathed on them and said, 'Receive the Holy Spirit.</u> If you forgive anyone his sins, they are forgiven; if you withhold forgiveness from anyone, it is withheld'"
(John 20:21-23)

"But <u>you will receive power when the Holy Spirit has come upon you</u>, and you will be my witnesses in Jerusalem and in all Judea and Samaria, and to the end of the earth"
(Acts 1:8)

Those are our foundational verses. Within them are several repeated terms and words. These are used by Jesus to help us understand our commission. We will break them into three parts, and then define and explain what each mean to us:

Part 1:
Power – Authority – The Kingdom of God – Being Sent

Part 2:
Healing – Deliverance

Part 3:
Preaching the Gospel

PART 1

CHAPTER 3
POWER & AUTHORITY

Following a Sunday morning service, I was invited to a Pastor's house that clung to the side of a very steep mountain in North East India. There were other pastors sat on one side of the room as I was praying for many of their parishioners on the other side of the room. These were godly, devout men, who had more ministry experience than myself. I could sense their great curiosity as I prayed for these people. Before their eyes they watched Jesus heal each person, it was beautiful.

One of the ladies could not talk properly, she only made grunts and sounds. She had suffered with pressure in her chest for many years and her speech was hindered. It was very difficult for her to try and explain her ailment. I could see that it was causing her discomfort so I offered to pray. I could discern by the Holy Spirit that this precious lady was troubled by a demon. I took authority over the demon and immediately she started speaking perfectly clear with no hindrance. Also, all the pain and pressure in her chest left. What was funny is that for the rest of the time that I was praying for everyone else, this lady did not stop talking. She obviously was wanting to make up for time lost. I can still hear her voice chirping in the background.

On another occasion, here in the US, I was asked to pray for a baby that had died. I went to the hospital and made my way to the room of the grieving parents. I had never prayed for a dead child before and it was heavy on my mind. When the baby boy was brought up to the ward, they placed the crib in another secluded room for me to go and pray for him. I prayed for about twenty minutes without any effect. I alternated between praying in tongues, calling for his soul by name to come back to his body, and speaking life to this lifeless child. After about twenty minutes the body began to vibrate. It was a low vibration, like a cell-phone vibration but slightly deeper, and wider, it is hard to describe. I thought the child was about to revive and I started to declare life with more enthusiasm. Then, to my dismay, three nurses burst through the door to pass through the room I was in, and we all looked shockingly at each other. I quieted down my prayers and within seconds the vibrations stopped. What lay before me was a lifeless child.

The rest of that day, and the next, I was sad. These were friends who had lost their baby whilst giving birth. I was grieving with them. As I was processing this difficult experience, I asked God why the body vibrated. I believe the Holy Spirit spoke these words to me:

"The power of life in you came in contact with death. The vibrations were because of that contact. A conflict of Kingdoms"

Some of us may have had encounters of praying for the sick where we will feel like *electricity* is moving through our hands, almost like a tingling in the hands. This is, like the story of the baby and the vibrations, evidence of the power of God moving through us. The above story of the lady who could not speak and was freed from a tormenting spirit is evidence of Jesus' authority moving through us. Knowing the difference between Power and Authority is vital for us as we go out because these were the two things that Jesus **GAVE** His apprentices.

Power:

"But you will receive power when the Holy Spirit has come upon you, and you will be my witnesses in Jerusalem and in all Judea and Samaria, and to the end of the earth"
(Acts 1:8)

The word here for power is the Greek word – **Dunamis**: Let us look at some different definitions:

- Power through God's ability - *dunamis* is needed in every scene of life to really grow in sanctification and prepare for heaven (HELPS Word-Studies)

- Inherent power, power residing in a thing by virtue of its nature (Good Power / Evil Power)

- The power of performing miracles: Acts 6:8 (READ) every kind of power of working miracles, physical power, force, might, ability

- Moral power and excellence of soul (Strong's Concordance)

- Overwhelming power of creation and miracles (Haglin)

When the Holy Spirit comes upon us, we are given power, we are empowered. It is power to BE witnesses and power to DO the works of God. **Power to BE and Power to DO!** If I were to define power in the context of ministry, I would say that:

Power is authority in action

Authority:

There are other Greek words for power and authority that help us understand that we are to both live lives that demonstrate His power and authority, and that we are to be sustained by His power and authority.

- *Energeia (En)*: The efficient harnessed release of power for controlled purpose, performance, or operation, such as changing a life or healing the sick.

- *Kratos (K)*: The power of effective government that takes command both within our personal lives and over the country; that conquers, rules and establishes a new order.

- *Ischuos (I)*: The might or muscle power that overcomes, binds up, and sets free; both physical and spiritual strength; power that overcomes the strong man and demons.

- *Exousia (Ex)*: Executive power, authority, and dominion. (Compiled by Paul & Gretel Haglin – Resurrection Christian Ministries – Used with permission)

Let us look at three portions of Scripture that contain all of the above Greek words. They show us the beautiful interplay between power and authority:

"...the eyes of your heart being enlightened, in order for you to know what is the hope of His calling, what are the riches of the glory of His inheritance in the saints, and what is the surpassing greatness of His power(D) toward us believing according to the working(En) of the power(K) of His might(I),which He worked(En) in Christ, having raised Him out from the dead, and having set Him at His right hand in the heavenly realms..."
(Ephesians 1:18-20)

"...for Yours is the Kingdom, and the power(D), and the glory,

forever and ever amen"
(Matthew 6:13)

"I <u>can do(I)</u> all things through him who strengthens me"
(Philippians 4:13)

Haglin paraphrases Philippians 4:13 this way:

"I have the physical and spiritual muscle power
to prevail in any demand coming upon me, through
Christ Jesus in me, my dynamic empowerer"

We cannot ignore this interplay between power and authority, it is vital for growing in our life with Christ and our earthly ministry. Simply put - Jesus empowers His apprentices.

For example, see how Jesus called the twelve disciples to Himself:

"And he went up on the mountain and called to him those whom he desired, <u>and they came to him</u>. And he appointed twelve (whom he also named apostles) so that they might be with him and he might send them out to preach and have <u>authority</u> to cast out demons"
(Mark 3:13-15)

Then a few chapters later we see Him sending them out:

"And he called the twelve and began <u>to send them out</u> two by two, and <u>gave them authority</u> over the unclean spirits…So they went out and proclaimed that people should repent. And they cast out many demons and anointed with oil many who were sick and healed them"
(Mark 6:7, 12-13)

In these two portions of scripture an important Greek word for authority is used:

- *Exousia*: - to be, being as a right or privilege – authority, delegated empowerment ("authorization"), operating in a designated jurisdiction. (HELPS Word-Studies)

Authority sets parameters in which power is to be exercised! That is why I explained that *Power is Authority in action*. **We live out of what we live in**. We live in a Kingdom of authority and move in power to demonstrate both the **Works of God (Power)** and the **Ways of God (Purity)**. Both our *Empirical* and *Ethical* positions are to display the influence and demonstration of His Kingdom rule:

- Empirical - based on experience rather than ideas (Oxford)
- Ethical - connected with beliefs and principles about what is right and wrong (Oxford)

Look at this verse concerning Jesus:

"And when Jesus finished these sayings, the crowds were astonished at his teaching, for he was teaching them as one who had authority(Ex), and not as their scribes"
(Matthew 7:28-29)

It is love, power and authority that make us to stand out.

How Authority Works:

Please just bear with me as I use a few, very simple examples, to explain how authority works. I wish to first start with a musical example.

Let me introduce you to the Whole Note:

The Whole Note can be broken down into other notes:

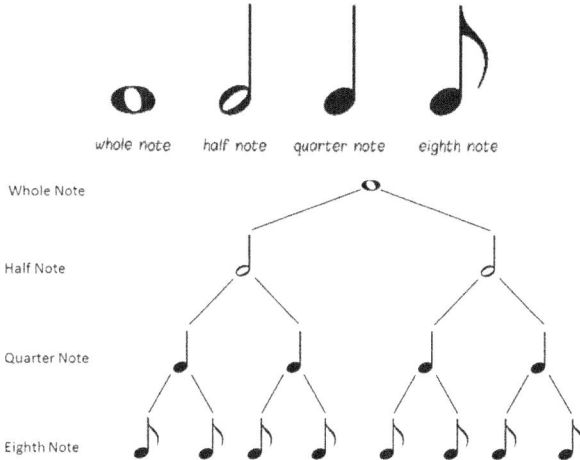

whole note   half note   quarter note   eighth note

Whole Note

Half Note

Quarter Note

Eighth Note

Each of these notes have a different length. They all come from the "Whole Note" but when broken up they each are distinct and necessary *(a Whole Note is made up of two "half notes", four "quarter notes", or eight "eighth notes", there are even 12^{ths}, 32^{nds}, 64^{ths}, 128^{ths} etc).*

Using this musical example, God is the composer. He has all authority. God then calls men and women, and with the commission comes authority. To one person he gives them a 64th note measure, another a quarter-note measure, and another a 16th note measure. We may not see the bigger picture but across creation, seen and unseen, God places everything in perfect symphonic order. God sees how all of the notes fit together:

Let me use another example. Just imagine a cake, or a pie:

God knows exactly what we need to complete a task. Let's say that the whole pie refers to the whole amount of authority given to a Pastor to complete their God-given assignment. The slices of the pie, either thick or thin, represent *"delegated"* authority. The Pastor will choose a Worship Leader, Administrator, Youth Pastor etc. Each are given a measure (slice) of authority that enables them to fulfill their tasks. Remember - **Authority sets parameters in which power is to be exercised.**

CHAPTER 4
AMAZING GRACE

With "Authority" comes "Responsibility", and with "Responsibility" we need "Grace". We are not talking about "Saving Grace" (Ephesians 2:8-9), but rather the ability that Jesus us gives us to live out our Christian lives and service.

One preacher said that:

> "Grace gives us the power to do what Truth demands"
> John Bevere

I've even heard Grace explained as:

> "God's operational power"

One Pastor said that:

> "Grace is the empowering presence of God that enables me to be who God created me to be, and to do all God created me to do"
> James Ryle

Basically:

Grace gives us the ability to do what we could not do before we received it! We cannot do His work without His Grace!

I remember the day that I was prayed for to be a Pastor. When our apostle laid his hands on me (Acts 6:6, 13:3, 14:23, 1 Timothy

4:14, 2 Timothy 1:6) I felt Grace fall on me like a cloak. It was in October of 2011. Equally, I remember the day that the Grace lifted for that role, I even remember where I was - March 2017, walking from my place of employment to my car! God changed everything in that short walk.

From that point on I did not have the stomach for leadership, and should've stopped all of our ministry activities immediately. It was complicated, because we still had a Saturday night service, and people were involved in our small Church. Instead, I continued for another year, and then had my first case of burnout.

After ending all Church services and midweek meetings, I went to Trucking School to be a Truck Driver in September 2018, but still kept one foot in ministry. In March 2019 after an exhausting and costly mission trip, I had another bout of burnout. Did I learn? Nope! I thought that I could still just let things coast along. I knew that there were some leaders, and their people in third world countries, that depended on our support. I assumed that I should continue.

In May 2020 I was done! I threw my Bible on the floor of my Truck. I was parked up at a truck stop in a town called Pioneer, Tennessee, feeling nothing like a pioneer. That night I fell asleep feeling sorry for myself. I had a dream that I was on a mission trip in the Philippines, and the Holy Spirit moved and refreshed me through that dream. I woke in the morning both revived and confused. I truly wanted to wallow for a few weeks, to feel sorry for myself, but the Lord would not allow it. He refreshed me. He spoke to me and I was strengthened (Ezekiel 2:2).

The million-dollar question is - Would this refreshing have happened in March 2017 if I had shut everything down then? I do not know. Or, did the Lord allow me to continue just to accentuate the point of His Grace? I do not know that either. What I do know - I do not want to do anything without His Grace. I've done it with and without, and with is better!

I'm sure you have similar experiences too. **We NEED His Grace to enable us to do what He has called us to do**. It all comes from Him, **the Call, the Commission, and the Charis** (Greek for

"Grace"). **Burnout occurs when we step outside of what we have Grace for.**

The apostle Paul said it like this:

> "But to each one of us grace has been given as Christ
> apportioned it"
> (Ephesians 4:7 NIV)

He would also write things like this:

> "For by the grace given to me I say..."
> (Romans 12:3)

It was the "grace" that empowered him to say things to people.

> "According to the grace of God given to me, like a skilled
> master builder I laid a foundation, and someone else is building
> upon it. Let each one take care how he builds upon it"
> (1 Corinthians 3:10)

The "grace" gave him the ability to lay foundations.

> "Having gifts that differ according to the grace given to us..."
> (Romans 12:6)

I truly love this. Paul was a minister who knew his boundaries and limitations. He even stated:

> "But we will not boast beyond limits, but will boast only with
> regard to the area of influence God assigned to us, to reach even to
> you"
> (2 Corinthians 10:13)

Authority brings Responsibility, and we need Grace to effectively carry out our God-given assignment.

CHAPTER 5
AUTHORITY AND
HEALING

Jesus' eternal words in Matthew 28:18 are extremely relevant to us:

> "All authority in heaven and on earth has been given to me..."

He has all authority and He has delegated authority to each of us according to the gifts, and grace, given us. Remember - *authority sets parameters in which power is to be exercised.* In the context of Jesus' words, it is leading people into the new life.

Even before His resurrection we see Jesus moving in healing. There are many examples to draw from, but since we are talking about authority let us focus on the account of the Roman Centurion:

> "When he had entered Capernaum, a centurion came forward to him, appealing to him, 'Lord, my servant is lying paralyzed at home, suffering terribly.' And he said to him, 'I will come and heal him.' But the centurion replied, 'Lord, I am not worthy to have you come under my roof, but only say the word, and my servant will be healed. For I too am a man under authority, with soldiers under me. And I say to one, 'Go,' and he goes, and to another, 'Come,'

and he comes, and to my servant, 'Do this,' and he does it.' When Jesus heard this, he marveled and said to those who followed him, 'Truly, I tell you, with no one in Israel have I found such faith…' And to the centurion Jesus said, 'Go; let it be done for you as you have believed.' And the servant was healed at that very moment" (Matthew 8:5-13)

From the Centurion's example I would like to highlight three points:

- **He came to Jesus** – When people come to you for prayer they've taken a big step, and hopefully have engaged their faith in Jesus, and believe that you are someone Jesus uses to heal people - Never forget this! **They are coming to who lives in you - Jesus!** It is an honor to pray for people. Sometimes the crowds will be big and it will take a lot of time to pray for them. But as my friend, Sunil, who is an evangelist in India, once said to me before I prayed for a large crowd of people, by myself – *"It is our privilege to pray for people!"*

- **He did not waste time** – This Soldier was on a mission. We must be those who are intentional when ministering. Don't waste people's time. It's not that we are "rushed", for we follow the Holy Spirit. Just be mindful to be intentional and engaged. A good rule-of-thumb is that - **We pray for results, or until the Holy Spirit tells us to stop**. Our ultimate confidence comes from God, not our level of experience. That's why we must learn to lean on His grace and not on our titles, or lack of titles. **Lean on His grace and great things will happen.** Give the burden of manifesting these things to the Holy Spirit. We lay our hands on people, He heals them!

- **His understanding of authority changed the outcome** – Jesus marveled that even His own Jewish brothers and sisters did not get this issue. The Centurion's understanding of authority helped his faith. **Authority is not in how loud we shout; authority is positional - "In Christ!"**

What's in your bag?

In Acts 3:1-10 we see the account of the paralyzed beggar at the gate called Beautiful. The famous phrase that Peter used was:

"I have no silver and gold, but <u>what I do have</u> I give to you. <u>In the name of Jesus Christ of Nazareth, rise up and walk!</u>"
(Acts 3:6)

There are no formulas in the New Testament for ministering to the sick, except maybe the laying on of hands (Mark 16:18), but even Jesus messed around with that one too. However, for this example, the laying on of hands is a constant, but the Scriptures show us that there are exceptions (Mark 7:32-35, Luke 17:11-19, John 9:1-7). Therefore, I must be open to exceptions. Sometimes we cannot lay hands on a person for whatever reason, but healing is still available. My point is that if there is a true formula when ministering to people, then it is being led by the Holy Spirit!

"<u>...filled with the [Holy] Spirit and constantly guided by Him</u>"
(Ephesians 5:18 AMP)

The Greek "present imperative tense" is used in this verse. It speaks of a *"continuous replenishment"*, **an ongoing state of being filled and guided**. The 1997 New Living Translation more accurately translates it:

"<u>Continually</u> being <u>filled and led</u> by the Holy Spirit"

How To Move in Authority & Power

Since the formula, or model, is a life full and led by the Holy Spirit, we also see from Acts 3:6 that **Peter _knew_ what he had!** I believe that Jesus' encouragement here is worth giving attention to:

> "And behold, I am sending the promise of my Father upon you. But stay in the city until you are clothed with power from on high"
>
> (Luke 24:49)

Please consider these three points:

- **KNOW** – It is important for us to know that we are empowered. Some have a reassurance in their spirits. Others physically feel His power. Whichever way it comes there must be a knowing. **We know, that we know, that we know!** I love the words of Heidi Baker, an apostle to Mozambique, concerning her own call - *"I know I have the cup, because He gave it to me. I know I have the bread, because He gave it to me!"*. The fruit of her ministry confirms her statement.

  What do you do if you are unsure whether you have "it"?

  We can lay hands on you to receive the Holy Spirit (Acts 8:17), that's Biblical. Or even during these training sessions, you can seek the Lord yourself and *"...wait until you are clothed with power from on high"*. Then I have seen others who do not feel a thing physically, or emotionally, but they just receive it by faith and stuff happens. As one preacher said – *"We live by faith, not feelings. We live by faith, and feelings follow"* – If you don't "feel" it, then move by faith, and eventually, your feelings usually confirm what you've done in faith. I believe that this is evidence of God bringing order, and wholeness, between our spirit, soul, and body. **(For explanation purposes - The Holy Spirit is not an "*it*", we are referring to "*it*" being *Power*, "*it*" being *Authority*. The "*it*" comes from Him, because when you have Him, or more accurately, when He has you, then you'll have "*it*")**

We cannot do effective ministry without this power, so make sure you know you have it to give away. Remember, it is not the Holy Spirit who baptizes us, it is Jesus (Mark 1:8, John 20:22), this again is proof that He is equipping us. In the Old Testament, when they were dedicating the Temple under King Solomon's reign, the Glory came so powerfully that the Priests could not minister (1 Kings 8:11). In the New Covenant, I believe, that it is impossible for us to minister without the Glory. **Under the Old Covenant the Glory *disabled* Priestly Ministry, but now, under the New Covenant the Glory *enables* Priestly Ministry!**

- **SHOW** – This is a "Show & Tell" Kingdom. If we know that we are empowered then it is to do the works of God (Mark 16:18-19, Ephesians 2:10). **Every believer** should be healing the sick, casting out demons, raising the dead, and performing miracles. The power is not for goosebumps, it is for shaking cities and nations and turning them upside down. It is the substance of God moving in and through us in ways that people cannot deny. Over a hundred times in the Bible the phrase *"Then you will know that I am the LORD"* is used (Exodus 6:7, Ezekiel 37:12-14, Joel 3:9-17). Most of the time it is used after God describes His powerful acts and works. For us today, this means that people are supposed to see the Power of God displayed in and through us to such a degree that they are left knowing that there is no god like God! As one preacher says **"We owe the world an** encounter with God!"

• **GROW** – a) We have several verses in the New Testament that show us that we are always meant to be using what we have, and increasing in what we have. The Parable of the Talents (Matthew 25:14-30, Luke 19:11-27) show us in detail that **what God gives us can increase**. This is how the realities of His reign come to bear through our lives (Isaiah 9:7). Also, this beautiful verse in 2 Corinthians 3:18 explains to us a wonderful truth – *"And we all, with unveiled face, beholding the glory of the Lord, are being transformed into the same image from one degree of glory to another. For this comes from the Lord who is the Spirit"* – As we yield to Him we will continue to grow (1 Timothy 4:16).

I have heard it taught that the way to grow in power is intimacy with Jesus. I do not fully agree with that. I believe the missing component is "obedience", **it's intimacy and obedience**. Evan Roberts, the 1904 Welsh Revivalist, regularly preached a four-point sermon of important things to do for things to be right between you and God. Point number three was *"Obey the Holy Spirit promptly"*. I read in a book by A.A. Allen that *"in a sense, it is all free, but there is a price of obedience and preparedness"*. Peter even said that the Holy Spirit is *"given to those who obey him (God)"* (Acts 5:32). This underscores so much of what will enable us to represent Him well to the nations. **He requires a people that He can trust to do what He says when He says it**. Our lives do not belong to us (1 Corinthians 6:19b), they are His. We are His servants, not the other way around!

b) Studying what the Word has to say about healing, deliverance, miracles etc. is great. Read the Gospels over and over and just see how Jesus lived, and live that out.

Absorb yourself in the testimonies of healing. Watch YouTube clips on miracles and healings. Read books on healing, even if you've been in ministry for a long time. Whenever I get to train Church leaders, I use this phrase to state two important realities - ***"Firstly, Keep Jesus before your eyes! Secondly, Keep Jesus before the eyes of the people!"*** He is in the miracles; He is in the testimonies, because it is all Him. By surrounding ourselves with such things we will feed our faith.

People of Power

We need that definite touch of His power on our lives. Before the Baptism of the Spirit Peter denied Christ, after the baptism of the Spirit He boldly proclaimed the Gospel on the Day of Pentecost (Acts 2). I also love this verse a few chapters later in Acts 8:1:

"And there arose on that day a great persecution against the church in Jerusalem, and they were all scattered throughout the regions of Judea and Samaria, <u>except the apostles</u>"

What had changed to make these disciples stand their ground? The Holy Spirit! When He comes, He comes in power.

Paul gives us such insight into this power:

"And I, when I came to you, brothers, did not come proclaiming to you the testimony of God with lofty speech or wisdom. For I decided to know nothing among you except Jesus Christ and him crucified. And I was with you in weakness and in fear and much trembling, and my speech and my message were not in plausible words of wisdom, <u>but in demonstration of the Spirit and of power, so that your faith might not rest in the wisdom of men but in the power of God</u>"
(1 Corinthians 2:1-5)

"Since you seek proof that Christ is speaking in me. <u>He (Christ) is not weak in dealing with you, but is powerful among you</u>. For

he was crucified in weakness, <u>but lives by the power of God</u>. For we also are weak in him, but in dealing with you we will live with him by the power of God. Examine yourselves, to see whether you are in the faith. Test yourselves. Or do you not realize this about yourselves, that Jesus Christ is in you?—unless indeed you fail to meet the test!"
(2 Corinthians 13:3-5)

In the New Testament there are two different forms of baptism of the Holy Spirit. Both forms can be found on the day of Pentecost. In Acts 2 Peter uses this phrase:

"…you will receive the gift of the Holy Spirit"
(Acts 2:38)

There is a picture of the Father extending His hand toward us and offering us the Holy Spirit, we must, by faith, take hold of the Holy Spirit for Him to take hold of us. That is valid!

The other example of the baptism of the Spirit is when He sovereignly falls. This happened in the upper room of Acts 2. The believers who had heeded Jesus' words from Luke 24:49 had waited in the city until they were clothed with power from high. But there is also another significant account in Acts of when Peter visited the house of Cornelius. This was the open door to the Gentiles that shifted the attention from just the Jews, to all humankind. Look at these verses:

"While Peter was still saying these things, the Holy Spirit fell on all who heard the word. And the believers from among the circumcised who had come with Peter were amazed, because the gift of the Holy Spirit was poured out even on the Gentiles. For they were hearing them speaking in tongues and extolling God. Then Peter declared, "Can anyone withhold water for baptizing these people, who have received the Holy Spirit just as we have?" And he commanded them to be baptized in the name of Jesus Christ. Then they asked him to remain for some days"
(Acts 10:44-48)

Amazing, look at that! *"While Peter was still saying these things, the Holy Spirit fell on all who heard the word"*, the Holy Spirit did not ask Peter if it was ok for Him to disrupt Peter's sermon, the Holy Spirit just fell on those in the room. Men, women, and children, whole families and friends!

The word *"fell"* in the original language means:

- *epipipto* - to fall upon; to rush or press upon, to seize, take possession of (Thayer's)

The Holy Spirit took possession of the Gentiles in that one event. It was so significant that when Peter returned to Jerusalem to testify concerning what had happened, he said:

"As I began to speak, the Holy Spirit fell on them just as on us at the beginning. And I remembered the word of the Lord, how he said, 'John baptized with water, but you will be baptized with the Holy Spirit.' If then God gave the same gift to them as he gave to us when we believed in the Lord Jesus Christ, who was I that I could stand in God's way?"
(Acts 11:15-17)

Their response is beautiful:

"When they heard these things they fell silent. And they glorified God, saying, 'Then to the Gentiles also God has granted repentance that leads to life'"
(Acts 11:18)

Concerning the word "silent", Thayer's New Testament Dictionary says it:

- describes a mental condition and its manifestation, especially in speechlessness (silence from fear, grief, awe, etc.)

The apostles needed a moment to take in the magnitude of

what Jesus had done at Cornelius' house. Then they glorified God. I love that. I wish that I was there!

Finally, to conclude this section, take a look at these two pictures. The first example, where we "receive the Holy Spirit" (Acts 2:28), may look something like this:

The second example of the Holy Spirit (Acts 10:44), concerning taking "possession" of a life, or "seizing" our life, He is like the player in the red picking up the player in the yellow and running with him,

OH LORD SEIZE OUR LIVES FOR YOUR PURPOSE!

CHAPTER 6
THE KINGDOM
OF GOD

It is not our purpose to provide a thorough teaching on the Kingdom here, but to speak of it in context of Jesus' commission. He has called us to preach that the Kingdom has come! Jesus said to His disciples that whenever they entered a city, town, or village:

> "...proclaim as you go, saying, 'The kingdom of heaven is at hand. Heal the sick, raise the dead, cleanse lepers, cast out demons'"
> Matthew 10:8

Look at your desk in front of you, or your table, or wherever you are. What is within reach of you? Your pen. Maybe a drink. Even a person sat next to you. Something that you can easily reach out and touch. That is what is meant by the phrase *"The Kingdom of heaven is at hand"*, it's within our reach! It's not a stretch, but within our immediate grasp.

In the above verse an interesting fact is that the preaching part was only **one-part of five things** that Jesus instructed His apprentices to do. This is why I took so long to focus on "Power" and "Authority" because this is how we prove and demonstrate the realities of His Kingdom. If I could say it like this –

The evidence that the Kingdom is at hand are the healings, resurrections, cleansings, and deliverances!

This requires a definition of the Kingdom in the context of Evangelism:

**The effects, and evidence, of His Rule,
to those who encounter Him.**

In any country there are borders. The ruling leader, say a King or Queen, or maybe a government represented by a President or Prime Minister, institute and enforce the laws of that country, and they apply from border to border. Also, within a country there are various customs and cultures unique to that country. Languages and dialects help the country to communicate. Trade and industry affect the wealth of a nation. These are all shadows of the Kingdom of God.

His Kingdom has no borders. God's King, Jesus, is seated on a throne in heaven (Isaiah 66:1). We are here on this earth as Ambassadors of His Kingdom (2 Corinthians 5:20). Just like the British Embassy in Johannesburg is British soil in another country, so too are we carriers of another Kingdom on this earth (John 17:14-19). **Wherever we go, we carry the soil of Heaven in our hearts, we are walking embassies. Where we go His Kingdom goes.** This fills us with such a sense of responsibility to represent His Kingdom. Whether we are in a restaurant, a prison cell, a market place, or a Church sanctuary, we are embassies. A.W. Tozer said that - "We live under a friendly sky". **As Believers we are not trying to open the heavens, we live under an open heaven as we move in Kingdom power and authority.**

Not only are healings, resurrections, cleansings, and deliverances evidence of the Kingdom, we also see some other wonderful bundles of fruit concerning the Kingdom in our lives.

"For the kingdom of God is not a matter of eating and drinking but of righteousness and peace and joy in the Holy Spirit"
(Romans 14:17)

"For the kingdom of God does not consist in talk but in power"
(1 Corinthians 4:20)

We can see that the evidence of **RIGHTEOUSNESS – PEACE – JOY – and POWER** in our lives, are also evidence of His Rule in, and through, our lives. I can look at my life and ask myself *"Am I growing and increasing in these areas?"* See, Isaiah 9:7 states that:

"Of the <u>increase</u> of his government and of peace there will be no end"

We should be expecting, and experiencing, the reality of this in our lives. The empirical and the ethical, works and ways, power and purity. His Kingdom increasing in us, and flowing from us (1 Corinthians 15:45).

When Jesus came to earth the Kingdom came (Matthew 2:2, John 18:37). The Kingdom comes when the King comes. It's not relegated to a future age. The Kingdom is NOW! It has COME, it is HERE, and it is COMING! We then are to be subject to that Kingdom. Paul wrote concerning what God has done for us,

"He has rescued us from the dominion of darkness and <u>brought us into the kingdom of His beloved Son</u>, in whom we have redemption, the forgiveness of sins"
(Colossians 1:13-14)

<u>**We are in the Kingdom**</u>, and we represent His Kingdom on this earth now, today! (1 Peter 2:9-12, Revelation 1:5-6, 5:10)

The effects of His Kingdom in our lives are a growing in righteousness, peace, joy, and power. The effects of His Kingdom flowing from our lives should be proclamations, healings, resurrections, cleansings, deliverances, good works, and kind deeds! <u>It is an internal spiritual ecosystem that affects the external world-system around us!</u>

This will affect our villages, towns, cities, and nations with

His peaceful government (Isaiah 9:7). We are called to disciple whole nations, not just the people living in them. **The Gospel of the Kingdom reaches to the Inhabitants and Infrastructures of nations.** It is much bigger than we give it thought or credit. We are bigger on the inside than we are on the outside. So, let His Kingdom come!

Being Sent

Before Jesus' resurrection, we have two groups in the scriptures that we have looked at. The twelve apostles, and the seventy-two other disciples. Out of however many were following Him He chose twelve men whom He also called apostles (noun – *apostolos* - Mark 3:14, Luke 6:13). He did not call the seventy-two other disciples "apostles" though. The twelve were to be His main team that He would pour a lot of His life and teaching into.

The Greek word for "apostle" is:

- *apostolos* - a messenger, one sent on a mission (Strong's)

Jesus is an apostle:

- "Therefore, holy brothers, you who share in a heavenly calling, consider Jesus, the apostle (*apostolos*) and high priest of our confession" (Hebrews 3:1)

- He was "Sent". Jesus said in John 20:21 - "Peace be with you. As the Father has sent (*apostelló*) me, so I am sending you"

In Mark's account concerning the twelve, we read:

"And he went up on the mountain and called to him those whom he desired, and they came to him. And he appointed twelve (whom he also named apostles - *apostolos*) so that they might be with him and he might send them out to preach and have authority to cast out demons"
(Mark 3:13-15)

Jesus had spent a night in prayer before calling and choosing these men. We must remember that Jesus only did what He saw the Father do (John 5:19). So, it is likely that He was praying all night as the Father showed Him those who would be the ones, out of a crowd of however many, who would take the message on. Jesus even said to God,

"Of those whom you gave me I have lost not one"
(John 18:9)

These men are sometimes referred to, historically, as the "Apostles of the Lamb" (Revelation 21:14). They were chosen by God, and given to Christ, which He gave to His Church for the foundational work of establishing the Church, and teaching things we still adhere to today (Acts 2:42).

This ministry of *apostles* continues today (Ephesians 4:11-14), **and emphasis must be made that <u>the apostles that have followed throughout history are in addition to the original twelve, but not part of those twelve because they stand unique as they walked, lived, and ministered with Jesus during His earthly ministry</u>** (Acts 1:21-22).

At Westminster Abbey, in London, there is a memorial to John and Charles Wesley, the founders of the Methodist Church. Inscribed on the monument are the words of Charles Wesley:

"God buries his workmen, but carries on his work"

Throughout history God has raised up men and women to carry on His apostolic work.

The apostle Paul and Apollos are just two examples, scripturally, of the continuance of this kind of ministry to the Church. It is important to note that even though Jesus had ascended He still was, and is, commissioning apostles to His Church as part of His heavenly ministry.

Paul's words explain a lot, concerning his own apostolic

ministry:

"Last of all, as to one untimely born, he appeared also to me"
(1 Corinthians 15:8)

Not everyone is this *kind* of apostle –
"And it was He who gave some to be apostles, some to be
prophets, some to be evangelists, and some to be pastors and
teachers"
(Ephesians 4:11 NASB)

It's interesting to note that the New American Standard Bible
uses the word "some" where others translate it as "the". The
original Greek translation is interchangeable, put in other words –

**Christ gave the office of an apostle (prophet,
evangelist, shepherd, and teacher), and he
gave some to fill this/these office(s).**

As we have already seen, Jesus differentiated between these
groups during His earthly ministry, and He still does through His
heavenly ministry. It is possible to be the verb *(apostelló)*, and *most*
of us are, without being the noun *(apostolos)*, which only applies
to some. The antonym for "some" is "many", and therefore many,
as in most, of us can be, and are sent *(apostelló)* into the world on
a mission, without us holding the office of an "apostle" *(apostolos)*
like a Peter or a Paul.

(As a *nerdy* side note - I asked someone, good at math, to break
the numbers down for me. We do not know how many were
following Jesus at the time that he called the 12 and the 72. Out
of however many were there, 84 people were called by Jesus. 12 to
be His apostles, and 72 to be messengers that went ahead of Him.
This is what my friend wrote:

84 were chosen.
**12 out of 84 is 12 divided by 84, multiplied by 100, which is
14.3%**

72 out of 84 is 72 divided by 84 multiplied by 100, which is 85.7%
It works out, roughly, that 1 in 7 of those called were apostles

These are the numbers representing those called by Jesus at that time. They do not reflect today's figures. My point is to say that I firmly believe that there are a lot less true Ephesians 4 ministries on this earth than the modern-day Church boasts. We have too many self-proclaimed apostles, prophets etc. and we would be wise to not chase titles. If only 1 in 7 were called by Jesus back then to hold *one* of the Ephesians 4 roles, that ratio would look completely different today, maybe even 1 in thousands, or 1 in ten thousands, in light of how many Believers are in the world today. As the saying goes "the numbers don't lie". Okay, *nerdy* side note finished)

The Role of the "Many"

We have looked at the mission of the twelve, **but equally the seventy-two other disciples were also sent on a mission**:

"After this the Lord appointed seventy-two others and sent them (*apostelló*) on ahead of him, two by two, into every town and place where he himself was about to go"
(Luke 10:1)

We can see that the seventy-two were sent (verb - *apostelló*) to the villages that Jesus was going to visit Himself. They went ahead of Him to prepare the way. That was *their* "Mission", **they had the same authority and power that the twelve had!**

Why do I point this out? A Pastor friend once said in a sermon:

"Only 3% of people will ever have a position in a Church or ministry. That means that 97% of people's ministry is living out the Gospel where they are"

I do not know where my Pastor friend got his statistics, honestly, but this is the plain reality of our earthly journey.

Whether you are a Pastor, Prophet, Doctor, Farmer, or Truck Driver, **we all get access to the same Power & Authority to represent the King and His Kingdom wherever we are.**

Our aim with Village To Village (V2V)© is to equip, empower, and send out believers to whichever harvest field God gives them. The reality is that only a small amount of you, if any in this class, Jesus will raise up to serve in the offices listed in Ephesians 4. That is not our decision, but His! The Church has to change the way she thinks about ministry. **It's not all about titles and platitudes, but hands and feet serving and moving.** Technically speaking:

We are all in "full-time" service, but we all
serve fully **in different areas of life**

So don't worry about "titles", just serve people wherever you are!

Finally, for the sake of some balance, you can also hold a full-time job and be an apostle, prophet etc. I have a dear friend in Pakistan and he works as a school teacher from Monday to Friday, but he also pastors a thriving Church, and has planted thirty other Churches. There is such grace on his life for that. I love his example! We always encourage our teams to be gainfully employed, unless it is evident that God is providing for them to give more time and energy to ministering in a particular mission field. I work full-time as a Truck Driver. It helps fund the ministry that I am called to do. I will drive Trucks until it becomes necessary for me to give more time to what God has called me to do. **Employment is a worthy provision of God, and should not be seen as a hindrance to ministry.** If we can see it this way:

Everything we do should be treated as worship
and service to God, then there is no line of
distinction, all is holy ministry (service)

I am wary of those preachers who refuse to get employment to help support their families. I had one Pastor who would beg all the time, as though I was his source of income. I told him to trust God to provide for him a job because there was no provision coming his way from heaven, that I could see.

He said to me:

> "If I get a job then the members of my church will think that I am not serious about leading the church. They will leave and go to another church"

I said,

> "Let them go! You have great needs and are always asking and begging for money, when it is within your power to earn income. Also, try teaching your people what the Bible teaches about working and employment, so they will understand that you working a job is an honorable thing, and not a sign of you being uncommitted to them"

Unfortunately, this man did not receive my counsel and he is still begging, and is still in great need. People, that does not glorify God! I understand that there is poverty and unemployment in nations, and that some nations are worse than others. We help where we can to support those in need. My comments to that man were not to be mean. But his heart was not right within himself. **It is good to work, and it is one of the ways God provides for us.** The apostle Paul, and his team, worked on principle in Thessalonica to deal with this very issue:

> "Now we command you, brothers, in the name of our Lord Jesus Christ, that you keep away from any brother who is walking in idleness and not in accord with the tradition that you received from us. For you yourselves know how you ought to imitate us, because we were not idle when we were with you, nor did we eat anyone's bread without paying for it, <u>but with toil and labor we worked night and day, that we might not be a burden to any of you.</u> It was not because we do not have that right, but to give you in ourselves an example to imitate. For even when we were with you, we would give you this command: If <u>anyone is not willing to work, let him not eat.</u> For we hear that some among you walk in

idleness, not busy at work, but busybodies. Now such persons we command and encourage in the Lord Jesus Christ to do their work quietly and to earn their own living. As for you, brothers, do not grow weary in doing good. <u>If anyone does not obey what we say in this letter, take note of that person, and have nothing to do with him,</u> that he may be ashamed. <u>Do not regard him as an enemy, but warn him as a brother</u>"
(2 Thessalonians 3:6-12)

Strong words from the apostle, but divinely inspired. God does not like idleness nor laziness. This problem has always been in the Church. My mentioning it is not to condemn anyone, but to encourage you to do what is righteous according to Scripture. If you can work, then work. There is a terrible misconception that not to work means to "live by faith". Many in our team work, and guess what? We are living by Faith. Maybe the workplace is the harvest field assigned to you. You may have been praying for "provision" to fulfill your ministry, well maybe the provision comes in the form of employment, and a pay check. I know it has for me, and others on our team. Maybe it will be for you also.

PART 2

INTRODUCTION – HEALING & DELIVERANCE

THE FOLLOWING NOTES, FOR PART 2, ARE TAKEN FROM A MANUAL PRODUCED BY RANDY CLARK, OF GLOBAL AWAKENING. THESE NOTES ARE USED WITH PERMISSION – ©2008 Global Awakening

TO PURCHASE PRAYER CARDS, OR LEARN MORE ABOUT THESE SUBJECTS, AND MANY OTHERS, PLEASE VISIT: WWW.GLOBALAWAKENINGSTORE.COM

OR VISIT THEIR MAIN WEBPAGE: WWW.GLOBALAWAKENING.COM

CHAPTER 7
MINISTRY OF
HEALING:
A FIVE-STEP
PRAYER MODEL

Lesson Goals

- Understand that this model is a proven starting place for every "little ole' me" to enter into healing ministry anytime and anywhere through the guidance and empowerment of the Holy Spirit.
- Learn a Five-Step Model for the ministry of healing.
- Learn practical ministry tips for operating in healing ministry.
- Be ready to step out and pray!

Introduction

In this lesson we will look at a Five-Step prayer model for praying for the sick.

The Five Steps are:

1. **The Interview.**
2. **The Diagnosis.**
3. **The Prayer Selection.**

4. **The Prayer Ministry (Pray for Effect).**
5. **Post-Prayer Suggestions.**

This model is not the only way to pray for healing, but is the model that has been taught and used by ministry teams at Global Awakening conferences, crusades, and international trips bearing powerful fruit in people's lives. It is quiet, loving, and effective. It can be used by anyone and anywhere-in the home; in the gathering of believers; and for reaching out into the streets, marketplace, and workplace!

Key Insights

Step One: The Interview:

"A man in the crowd answered, "Teacher, I brought you my son, who is possessed by a spirit that has robbed him of speech. Whenever it seizes him, it throws him to the ground. He foams at the mouth, gnashes his teeth and becomes rigid. I asked your disciples to drive out the spirit, but they could not. So they brought him. When the spirit saw Jesus, it immediately threw the boy into a convulsion. He fell to the ground and rolled around, foaming at the mouth. Jesus asked the boy's father, "How long has he been like this?" "From childhood," he answered"
(Mark 9:17-18, 20-21)

Briefly interview the person requesting prayer. *Be attentive and gentle.* A loving attitude on your part will do much to reassure the person that he or she is in good hands.

Ask the person what the physical need is, but do not go into lengthy detail.

For example:

- "What is your name?" (A question or two to put the person at ease.)
- "What would you like prayer for?"
- "How long have you had this condition?"
- "Do you know what the cause is?"

- "Have you seen a doctor?" "What does he say is the matter?"
- "Do you remember what was happening in your life when this condition started?"
- "Did anything traumatic happen to you about the time your condition began, or within a few months prior to it starting?"

[You may need to explain to the prayee why you are asking these last two questions]

This is often sufficient for the initial interview. You may now know the nature and cause of the condition. In some cases you won't know, so ask the Holy Spirit for His leading and maybe ask additional questions. If His leading isn't clear to you, you must make an educated guess as to the nature and cause of the condition.

Step Two: The Diagnosis:

The goal of the diagnosis is to answer the question, *"What is the root cause of this sickness or infirmity?"* (NOTE: We use the term diagnosis in the sense of "how to pray." We are NOT speaking of natural, medical diagnosis. While we seek from the prayee to understand what they are aware of in this area during the interview process of Step One, medical diagnosis is properly the domain of trained, licensed professionals.) The purpose is so that we may better understand HOW TO PRAY.

If you now know the cause of the condition, go at once to "Step Three: Prayer Selection."

Possible roots may be:

- An afflicting spirit.
- Sickness of the soul, psychosomatic.
- Natural cause, such an accident, break, cut, or other injury.
- A violation of God's laws for living.

Some examples:

- Perhaps there was an accident, which would usually suggest a natural cause. (But, he may need to forgive the person who caused the accident. This could mean himself, if he caused it.)
- Perhaps the person was born with the condition, which would often suggest a natural cause, or possibly a generational curse.
- The condition may be partly or totally caused by emotional stress.
  Perhaps the person has had headaches ever since he lost a job.
  Perhaps his back has hurt ever since someone cheated him.
  Perhaps cancer was discovered a few months after a divorce, or after the death of a parent or child.
- The cause might be spiritual: Perhaps the person has had nightmares since an occult experience he had. Perhaps his condition is the result of a habitual sin. Perhaps it is the effect of a curse of some kind.

As noted above, if the cause is not known, ask the Holy Spirit for His leading as to the nature and possible cause of the condition. You may want to go back to the interview stage and ask further questions.

Step Three: The Prayer Selection:

The ultimate goal here is to PRAY FOR EFFECT. So, led by the Holy Spirit, select the prayer ministry to be most effective in dealing with the specific need(s).

Types of ministry:

a) **Petition: A request to heal, addressed to God, to Jesus, or to the Holy Spirit.**

For example:

- "Father, in the name of Jesus I ask you to restore sight to this eye."
- "Father, I pray in Jesus' name, come and straighten this spine."
- "Father, release Your power to heal, in Jim's body, in the name of Jesus."
- "Come, Holy Spirit. Release your power. Touch Jim's back, in Jesus' name."

b) **Command: A command addressed to a condition of the body, or to a part of the body, or to a troubling spirit, such as a spirit of pain, infirmity, or of affliction**

A command is appropriate:

- As your initial step, unless you are led otherwise by the Holy Spirit.
- When there has been a word of knowledge for healing, or some other indication that God wants to heal the person at this time.
- When petition prayers have been tried and progress has stopped.
- When casting out an afflicting spirit, or any other spirit.
- When a curse or vow is broken.
- Whenever you are so led by the Holy Spirit.

For example:

- "In the name of Jesus, I command this tumor to shrivel up and dissolve."
- "In the name of Jesus, spine, be straight! Be healed!"
- "In Jesus' name, I command every afflicting spirit, get out of Jim's body."
- "In the name of Jesus, I command all pain and

swelling to leave this ankle.

Preliminaries to praying for healing itself:

1. Forgiveness of another's wrong conduct.

Unforgiveness can be a major obstacle to healing. If it appears that someone else caused the condition, or that someone wronged the person about the time the condition started, find out if the sick person has forgiven the other. If not, forgiveness should precede your prayer for healing.

Examples:

- A woman has had arthritis in her spine for five years, ever since her husband ran off with another woman. Has she forgiven her husband and the woman? Jesus said we must forgive, not we ought to. Emotional stress can cause illness, prevent healing. Sometimes one can be angry at God and must forgive Him.

- A pastor has had back pain for ten years. Ten years ago there was a split in his church and some of his closest friends turned against him. Has he forgiven the ringleaders of the split, his former friends, and all others involved?

Note: Sometimes a person is healed before you even begin to pray for healing, just by forgiving the person who caused the hurt, or just by repenting and asking God's forgiveness for his own sin of resentment and anger. The pastor noted above was healed by forgiving, without any prayer for healing.

2. Repentance for one's own wrong conduct, and asking forgiveness for it.

If it appears that the condition was brought on by sin, very gently inquire if the person agrees that this might be so. If he does, encourage him to repent and ask God's forgiveness. This should precede your prayer for healing. Sin that is not repented of can impede healing.

Be tender. Ask if perhaps the condition could be related to his lifestyle, or perhaps say, "I wonder if this condition could be related to things you have done in the past." **<u>NEVER accuse the person confrontationally of causing his condition by his sin.</u>**

If this leading is of the Holy Spirit, the Holy Spirit will usually indicate the specific sin which is the problem, not sin in general.

General accusations of sin are often destructive, and probably are from the enemy.

A person may need to forgive himself or herself from having caused the the injury or sickness. This may seem unnecessary, but it sometimes releases healing.

Some examples:

- Anger can contribute to back pain and some depressions.
- AIDS might have resulted from a wrong lifestyle.
- Lung cancer might have been caused by smoking.

3. **An attitude of receiving.**

- **Ask the person not to pray while you are praying for him.**
  Here again, be gentle and loving, and say something like: "I know this means a lot to you, and you have probably prayed a lot about your condition. But for now I need you to focus on your body. I want you to just relax and to let me know if anything begins to happen in your body.

- **Sometimes a person may find it very hard not to pray.**
  <u>Don't be hung up on this</u>. Pray for the person anyway!

Now that the preliminaries are over, it is time for the actual prayer ministry!

Step 4: The Prayer Ministry (Praying for Effect):

"When Jesus saw that a crowd was running to the scene, <u>he rebuked the evil spirit. "You deaf and mute spirit," he said, "I command you, come out of him and never enter him again." The spirit shrieked, convulsed him violently and came out..."</u>
(Mark 9:25-26)

Now is the time to pray. **At this point you will want to pray according to the prayer selection made in the previous step**. Remember the goal was to select a prayer to effect healing and/or deliverance!

Following is a discussion of things to keep in mind during prayer ministry.

1) Audibly ask the Holy Spirit to come.

You can say simply, "Come, Holy Spirit!" Or, "Come, Holy Spirit, with Your healing power."

If the presence of the Holy Spirit becomes evident, as by the person feeling heat, tingling, or some other manifestation, continue waiting on Him until He finishes what He wishes to do at that time. When the manifestation has ebbed, check to see if healing is complete. If it is not complete, continue your ministry.

2) Remember to always pray or command in the name of Jesus.

"And these signs will accompany those who believe: In my name they will drive out demons; ... they will place their hands on sick people, and they will get well"
(Mark 16:17a, 18b)

You cannot use the name of Jesus too much! The power is in His name. Some who have anointed healing ministries sometimes simply repeat "In the name of Jesus", over and over as their prayer for healing.

3) Thank God for whatever He does.

"And whatever you do, whether in word or deed, do it all in the
name of the Lord Jesus, giving thanks to God the Father through
him"
(Colossians 3:17)

This honors the person and presence of the Holy Spirit and
the Name of Jesus. You cannot thank God too much! Many times
during worship and thanksgiving the level of healing power
increases.

4) Keep prayers or commands short.

If changes in the seeker's condition can be readily determined,
it is appropriate and often helpful to pray short prayers or give
brief commands, interspersed with re-interviewing at frequent
intervals to see if progress is being made:

- "Are you better?"
- "Did you feel anything?"
- "Are you still feeling anything?"
- "What has happened to the pain now?"
- "Did you feel any pain while I was praying?"
- "Did the pain move?"
- "See if you can read the sign now."
- "Do you still feel heat in your stomach?"
- "Try moving your knee now."

Note: A person may be partially or completely healed without
feeling anything. He may not realize that healing has taken place
until he uses the affected part. If he does something he could not
do before, or that caused pain before, he can see if the prayer thus
far has made a difference.

5) When a prayer or command results in a partial healing, continue to use it until you find that it no longer produces further healing.

If you try one kind of prayer or command and get results, but not complete healing, continue. Explain why you are continuing, for the person receiving prayer may wonder about the repetition. If you try one kind of prayer or command and get no result after a few times, try another kind! Be persistent

6) Consider whether further interviewing may reveal hindrances to healing.

"They came to Bethsaida, and some people brought a blind man and begged Jesus to touch him. He took the blind man by the hand and led him outside the village. When he had spit on the man's eyes and put his hands on him, Jesus asked, "Do you see anything?" He looked up and said, "I see people; they look like trees walking around." Once more Jesus put his hands on the man's eyes. Then his eyes were opened, his sight was restored, and he saw everything clearly"
(Mark 8:22-25)

If after a time you are making no progress, consider interviewing the person farther.

Possible questions might be:

- "Would you try again to remember whether anything significant happened within six months or so of the beginning of this condition?" (Some event may require forgiveness that the person may have forgotten or may have been unwilling to disclose.)
- "Do any other members of your family have this condition?" (If so, perhaps there is a generational spirit affecting several members of the family.)
- "Do you have a strong fear of anything?" (Fear can be a cause of many physical and spiritual problems, and it sometimes interferes with healing.)
- "Is anyone in your family a member of the Freemasons or Eastern Star?" (Association with Masonic or other occult organizations is particularly

likely to impede healing.)

- "Has anyone ever cursed you or your family that you know of?"
- "Have you had other accidents?" (If the person is accident-prone, consider whether he is under a curse.)
- "Have you ever participated in any kind of occult game or practice?"

7) Your manner

- **You need not necessarily pray aloud all the time.**
  If you wish, tell the person that you may pray silently at times, that as long as you have your hand on his arm you are praying, even if not aloud. And do pray silently. And listen to the Holy Spirit. He may give you some guidance you would otherwise miss.

- **It is often very helpful to pray with your eyes open, and observe the person you are praying for.**
  Look for signs that God is at work in his body: fluttering eyelids, trembling, perspiration. If you see something happening, or if the person reports a change in the pain, increased sight, or other progress, thank God for what He is doing, and bless it, and continue to pray in the manner that led to the progress.

- **Use your normal tone of voice.**
  Shouting, or praying loudly in tongues, will not increase your effectiveness.

- **Don't preach, don't give advice, and don't prophesy.**
  You job is to listen to the Holy Spirit and be a vessel of healing and deliverance!

8) Do everything in love.

If all is done in love, then even if the person is not healed, they can leave encouraged, loved, and full of hope, ready to come back for more prayer!

"Let all that you do be done with love" (1 Cor. 16:14 RSV)
"Love is patient... kind... not jealous...not arrogant or rude" (1 Cor.13:4 RSV)
"Love is not anxious to impress ...not touchy" (1 Cor. 13:4-5 Phillips)

9) Ministry to a person with multiple problems.

- **As a general rule, it is better to finish praying for one condition before starting to pray for another, unless the Holy Spirit directs you differently.**
  Flitting from one problem to another is distracting, and **the person's faith will be built up for successive problems if one healing is completed**. The sick person may ask you to pray for a second problem as soon as you finish your first prayer for one condition. He may not understand that you will pray further for the first condition. Tell him gently that you will pray for the second condition, but first you wish to finish praying for the first condition.

- **Follow the leading of the Holy Spirit!**
  If you are praying for a person's sinus infection, and his bad foot begins to tingle, stop praying for the sinus condition and pray for the foot. Bless what God is doing, and pray in cooperation with what He is doing. Go back to the sinus only when you have finished praying for the foot, or when the sinus begins to manifest the presence of God at work there.

10) Ministry to a person under medication.

Sometimes a person under medication (such as for diabetes, asthma, arthritis, heart disease, etc.) believes he has been healed when you pray for him. He may think he can discontinue his medication. You must instruct him to continue his medication after your ministry to him, even if he believes and even if you believe he has been healed. Have the person return to the doctor and let the doctor change or withdraw medication. If they are tested and no longer need it, it will be a testimony to God's healing power.

11) Stop praying when:

- The person is completely healed.
- The person wants you to stop. He may be tired or simply feel you should stop.
- The Holy Spirit tells you it is time to stop.
- You are not given any other way to pray, and you are not gaining ground.

Step Five: Post-Prayer Suggestions:

It is always important to follow up the prayer session with final encouragement and/or instructions.

- **Encourage the prayee's walk with the Lord:**
  You might share a scripture verse. For some people, scriptural passages are extremely meaningful and encouraging.

- **If a condition resulted from occult experiences or habitual sin, suggest tactfully that a change in lifestyle may well be needed to avoid a recurrence of his condition.**

- **If he is not healed, or not completely healed, don't**

accuse him of lack of faith for healing, or of sin in his life as the cause.

Encourage the person to get prayer from others if there is little or no evidence of healing, or if his healing has not been completed. Encourage him to come back again for more prayer after the next meeting, etc. Sometimes healing is progressive, and sometimes it occurs only after a number of prayers for healing have been made.

- **Tell the prayee not to be surprised if he experiences a spiritual attack after a healing, and help him to be prepared to resist it.**

  If a symptom starts to recur, he can command it to leave in Jesus' name. If a bad habit is involved, he may be tempted for a short time to re - commence the habit. If he does yield, quick repentance is needed and asking God's help.

CHAPTER 8
DELIVERANCE:
A TEN-STEP MINISTRY MODEL
BY PABLO BOTTARI

Session Goals

- To understand the Pablo Bottari Ten-Step deliverance model, so as to peacefully and lovingly participate in the ministry of deliverance (liberation).

Introduction

"So his fame spread throughout all Syria, and they brought him all the sick, those afflicted with various diseases and pains, those oppressed by demons, epileptics, and paralytics, and he healed them"
(Matthew 4:24)

"And these signs will accompany those who believe: in my name they will cast out demons; they will speak in new tongues"
(Mark 16:17)

In this session we will take what we have already learned about the New Testament reality of deliverance, and build on it by discussing specifics for moving in deliverance ministry. We want to emphasize that "seeing a demon under every bush" or behind every problem is not Biblical. But neither is the denial of their existence or operation. Sadly, many who could be helped, especially in Western societies, are denied assistance because of the lack of practical instruction or by theologies which deny their need. (One can read accounts of western missionaries have quickly changed their theology when confronted openly by demonic activity on the field in Asia, Africa, and South America.)

To review, deliverance is setting a person free from the oppression of a demonic spirit.

Note: the term "oppression" is used here, rather than "possession", because "possession" implies ownership and complete control. Since a believer has been purchased by the Lord Jesus Christ he cannot be "possessed" by Satan or his emissaries. However, many believers have been host to demonic presences in their years before conversion, and these evil spirits do not always cease operation against them when their host is converted.

For years, Pablo Bottari supervised the deliverance tent at evangelist Carlos Anacondia's crusades in Argentina. There he supervised deliverance ministry to many thousands, and personally participated in the deliverance of many hundreds of people, mostly believers. He felt that the deliverance ministry he saw at first was noisy, difficult, lengthy and often humiliating to the person being ministered to.

He developed a ten-step model for deliverance which is quietly effective. The model discussed in this session is based on his. It is quiet, pastoral, loving, non-humiliating, and very effective. It is followed in all Global Awakening crusades, conferences, international trips, and in many churches.

The Pablo Bottari Deliverance Model

Presuppositions:

- We're ministering to the person, not the demon.

- Authority, not wrestling, is the focus.
- Counseling, bringing the truth is key; quietness, is better than flamboyant demonstrations of warfare.
- It is extremely important to find out the entry points, the "open doors" and how to close those doors.
- They don't have to "throw up" or be torn or tormented to be delivered. Satan loves to make a scene. We want to rob him of that opportunity.

The Model's Ten Steps:

The following ten steps are followed in a session where the minister does not know the host person well, such as in most cases in a crusade or other public meeting setting. In some settings, some of these steps might be omitted. For example, where the minister knows the prayee is a believer and really wants to be set free, steps 4 and 5 would be omitted. If there is no manifestation during the ministry, step 2 and probably step 3 would be omitted.

Remember: These steps are a model, a guide. Pray for the guidance of the Holy Spirit at all times!

Step 1 - Give the individual priority:

- **Keep a loving attitude, not a militant attitude.**
Firmness is necessary in casting out a demon, but in the meantime, the prayee needs to feel loved and accepted.

- **Be encouraging. Raise hope.**
Emphasize to the prayee that Jesus can bring them freedom.

- **Don't emphasize the power of the demon; it is subject to you in the name of Jesus.**
Remember that the prayee may have been in bondage

for years, and perhaps has received many prayers that were not completely effective.

Step 2 - If a spirit manifests, bring it under submission, in the name of Jesus:

- **Take authority over the spirit.**
  Tell it, "Submit, in the name of Jesus!", or "Be quiet, in Jesus' name!" or similar commands. It is best to let the prayee know that you are not speaking to them, but to the demon.

- **Repeat such commands until the spirit is quiet.**

- **Don't be surprised if this takes time. Be persistent.**
  You may have to command the spirit several times – or even many times - - to submit. However, it will come under submission.

- **If others gather while you are quieting the spirit, ask them not to touch the prayee, and not to speak or pray loudly.**
  Your objective is not to keep the spirit stirred up, but to get the spirit to be quiet so you can talk to the prayee.

Step 3 - Establish and maintain communication with the prayee:

- **You must be able to talk with the person receiving ministry, because you must have his cooperation if the deliverance is to be successful.**

- **If you are not sure the prayee can hear you, ask— even if the person's eyes are closed.**

- **Maintaining communication may require additional commands to the spirit to submit, during ministry.**
  The prayee may drop his head, may close his eyes, or his eyes may wander. Ask him to hold his head up, to open his eyes, to look at you. If the person cannot do these things, a spirit is involved and you then order the spirit to submit.

Step 4 - Ask the prayee what he/she wants to be free from, and try to make sure he/she really wants to get free:

- **In a crusade situation, ask the person receiving ministry what he wants to be freed from.**
  If the prayee is uncertain, ask them what the speaker was praying about when the spirit started to manifest. Other helpful initial questions are whether he is trying to break any habit without success, or whether he has any conduct he considers odd or unusual.

- **In private ministry, the prayee probably will know what the bondages are that he or she wants to be set free from.**
  This can include one or two specific bondages, or it may involve a broader ministry – a thorough housecleaning. The prayee may have communicated this information in advance to the person who will be ministering.

- **If the prayee indicates that he does not want ministry even though a spirit has manifested, abide by that decision.**

- **If the prayee wants to leave after partial ministry, allow the person to leave.**

You may encounter attitudes that indicate lack of desire for complete freedom.

- **Do NOT try to detain the prayee or to minister against his or her will.**

Step 5 - Make sure the prayee understands to make Jesus Christ Lord and Savior:

- **The ministry recipient will need the help of the Holy Spirit to stay free.**
  If he is not a Christian, he probably will be back in bondage shortly, even if he is delivered. This should be explained to him. It isn't wise to try to deliver him in the hope that he will become a believer as a result of getting free.

"When an evil spirit comes out of a man, it goes through arid places seeking rest and does not find it. Then it says, 'I will return to the house I left.' When it arrives, it finds the house unoccupied, swept clean and put in order. Then it goes and takes with it seven other spirits more wicked than itself, and they go in and live there. And the final condition of that man is worse than the first. . . ."
(Matthew 12:43-45a)

- **If you can lead the person to Christ, do. If you can't, pray for him; bless him.**
  Pray for the healing of his hurts and wounds. Let him know by your attitude that you are not offended. Be loving. But don't cast out any spirits. Explain why you don't—because he won't be able to stay free. Encourage him to take the step of making Jesus his Lord and then return for deliverance.

Step 6 - Interview the prayee to discover the event or events, the conduct, or the relationship situations that have led to his/her bondage or bondages.

- **The purpose is to expose where forgiveness is required, and where healing, repentance and breaking of bondages are needed**

- **Find all open doors. If there is no obvious place to start, begin with his parental relationships, then move to other areas. Be thorough, don't rush.**

- **Do not stir up demons, keep them quiet. List the spirits encountered and areas requiring forgiveness of others or repentance.**

- **Consider a curse if the person has persistent difficulty in an area of life.**

- **Fear is an entry point for many different spirits (and a problem in many illnesses).**

Step 7 - Lead the prayee in "closing" these "doors" to the admission of spirits:

- **Forgive whoever caused the hurt or led him into wrong conduct.**

- **Repent and ask forgiveness for specific sins.**
  It is important to be specific, such as, "Father, forgive me for ___(hate, bitterness, sharing my body with ____, reading horoscopes etc.)"

- **Renounce all sins or spirits involved in the name of Jesus.**

• Renunciation should be audible and firm.

• Renunciation is not a prayer to God. It is spoken to the spirit involved, who is an enemy. It should be spoken as a command to an enemy, not a petition to God.

• Spirits taken in without the sin of the prayee need to be renounced the same as those that entered through his wrong attitudes or other fault. (For example, if a child witnesses his parents fighting (verbally or physically), he may take in spirits of confusion, anxiety, fear, insecurity, and others.)

• Renounce all spirits involved, in the name of Jesus. In the case of sex outside marriage, the person should renounce spirits taken in from every partner he can recall, individually by first names if possible.

• Pacts with Satan and inner vows must be renounced and curses broken:

  a. *"In the name of Jesus I renounce the spirits of _____ and _____."*
  b. *"In the name of Jesus, I renounce the vow I made never/always to_____."*

• **The minister should break the yoke of bondage and the power of any spirit.**
This closes the door. You or the seeker can do this:

• *"In the name of Jesus I break the power of the spirit(s) of _____ over (person's name) so that when they are cast out, they will not come back."*

> • *"In the name of Jesus I break the power of every curse over (person's name) from _____ (father's careless critical words, mother's rejection, etc.)"*

Step 8 - When all doors are closed, cast out the unclean spirit or spirits:

With all doors closed, the spirits will leave quickly and quietly. If they don't leave promptly, go back to Step 6. Tell the person there may be other spirits to deal with. Re-interview. Ask the Holy Spirit to show you or the seeker or a team member what He wants to do next.

Step 9 - Lead the prayee in a prayer of praise and thanksgiving to Jesus for his/her deliverance:

If the person cannot speak, or if spirits manifest, more doors need to be closed.

Step 10 - Have the prayee ask the Holy Spirit to fill him/her, to fill up every space formally occupied by an evil spirit:

We don't want to leave the house swept clean and empty! Spend time praying for an infilling of the Holy Spirit! You want them to leave in love with Jesus and rejoicing in HIS strength, power, and love!

Post ministry suggestions:

- **Walking in forgiveness as a lifestyle.**
  Explain that forgiveness is a decision, not a feeling, and that he can forgive a person even if he doesn't feel like it. He can choose to forgive. His spirit can have the rule over his emotions, and it is important to forgive for his own best interest.

  The prayee needs to know that the forgiveness process – of needing to forgive the same person more than once (sometimes many times) – is normal and not a sign that the deliverance ministry was a failure.

- **Asking the Lord for healing quickly after being hurt.**

- **Instruct them to commit to accountability, such as in an accountability/cell /home group in the person's local fellowship.**

- **Suggesting ways to change crucial habit patterns. Some possibilities are:**

Praise God, singing or listening to praise songs, reading Psalms.

Pray in his tongues

Take authority over tempting spirits in the name of Jesus and send them away.

Thank God for having been set free. THIS IS VERY IMPORTANT!!!

If he falls, he can repent quickly and get the door closed again.

If Satan accuses him of being a sinner, he can say: "You're right, Satan. Just look at what Jesus has forgiven me for!"

He can look for ways to remind himself that Jesus is his Lord. You can tell him that a number one priority should be to make Jesus the Lord over every area of his life.

Ask daily for infilling of the Holy Spirit.

- **Taking authority over any spirits that may try to attack or torment him/her again in the future.**

- **Praying in tongues.**

- Daily Bible reading, having intimate quiet time with God.

- Things that the Holy Spirit may prompt concerning walking in the light.

PART 3

CHAPTER 9
PREACHING THE
GOSPEL

What a task we have to convey this wonderful message to the world. I'd like to share this story that one of my Youth Pastors told me when I was teenager. This is the gist of the story.

He and a friend were walking around a particular neighborhood to "share the Gospel" and they came across a man, with a cast on his arm, who was trying to cut the grass in his yard. They approached the fence to engage the man. They started to share the Gospel and the other man with him said this phrase that really confused and angered the man with the cast on his arm:

"I was once lost in the world like you, but then I was washed in the blood of the Lamb and now I am saved"

The man made a very good point:

"What on earth are you talking about? Washed in the blood of the Lamb? That sounds weird. If you really wanted to help me you could cut my grass for me because my arm is hurting. Go away and leave me alone"

The Bible, and Christian jargon "Christian-ese", is a lost language to the average person on the streets. So how do we share the Gospel effectively? On the Day of Pentecost somebody in the crowd made an interesting statement:

"And we all hear these people speaking in our own languages about the wonderful things God has done"
(Acts 2:11 NLT)

The crowds may have been confused by the 120 people walking around like they were drunk. Also, there was an incredible sound that drew the whole city to this one house that had an upper room. Despite all of the supernatural occurrences, they were able to clearly understand the testimony concerning the wonderful things God has done! **That is our challenge!** We will see many sick people healed, many delivered from demons, and many other signs and wonders. However, we must convey the Goodness (Gospel) of God in a way that they understand.

For us, in the context of how we will be going Village To Village(V2V)© the two main techniques that we will use shall be SIGNS and STORIES!

Signs:

As we have already mentioned many times - the evidence of our Proclamation is the Demonstration of **healings, deliverances, resurrections, cleansings, good works, kind deeds etc!** They always speak for themselves.

In addition to the healing, deliverances etc. we must be open to "Signs and Wonders". Someone once asked *"What are Signs and Wonders?"* and the preacher answered *"Well a 'Sign' points to something. God will do something that will point to His Son. Sometimes these 'Signs' make you 'Wonder' what on earth does it all mean?"*

I heard a story about the late great Healing Evangelist T.L. Osborn's wife, Daisy. She was in a village in Africa. She stood in front of a Witch Doctor with a tree branch in her hand. God had told her to throw it to the ground. The branch turned into a snake, and then she picked the snake up and it turned back into a branch. The Witch Doctor accepted Jesus Christ immediately and the whole village came to Christ. That is a Sign and a Wonder.

I just read about a missionary couple to India who were tied to a tree while the village chief prepared a fire to cook them on. Suddenly the village chief experienced pain in his stomach and was rolling on the floor. Nobody knew what to do. The missionary man said "If you untie us, I can do something to help him", and they untied him and the missionary prayed for the village chief and he got instantly healed. They then led him to Jesus, he and the village.

I could tell you so many stories, and you probably have many you could tell, of strange things that God does as Signs that point to Jesus. We must be ready for them. They help us proclaim and demonstrate the Gospel!

Raising The Dead:

When I was teenager, if I were in a hospital, I would go and stand by the morgue and lay my hands on the wall, or the door, and call the dead to rise. I don't think anyone came back to life, because no one ever came out to tell me, or thank me. It was my youthful zeal that drove me to do things like that. Even today, I will still pray for a dead bird or animal, why? Because we don't always have opportunity to pray for dead people. I want to be ready! **Today it may be a dead bird but tomorrow it could be someone's child, spouse, or family member**. What I have learned, just like with demons, we don't go looking for the dead. We deal with whatever comes across our path. To date I have not seen someone raised from the dead, YET!

However, I would like to offer some guidelines that may help if you are confronted with the need to raise someone from the dead, gleaned from those who have raised the dead:

- **Seek the Holy Spirit:** Not everyone dies at the right time. Some die before their time. So how can you tell the difference? By asking the Holy Spirit. This is truly the most important step in this process.

- **Give it time:** I got to spend time with a man in South Africa who used to be one of Reinhard Bonnke's evangelists. He had seen six people raised from the dead at the point I met him. Pastor Robert told me that the first time he saw someone raised from the dead the whole village was waiting outside the door to kill him if the young girl did not come back to life. He said that he had a lot of pressure on him to raise that dead girl. It took six hours of prayer before she came back to life. On another occasion, at one of Bonnke's crusades, one of the women in the choir had fallen off the stage and hit her head on a rock and died instantly. Bonnke asked Pastor Robert to pray for the woman. Two hours later the woman came back to life. Finally, there is a missionary in Mexico called David Hogan. He himself has been used by God to raise over 37 people from the dead, and his ministry team have seen hundreds of people raised from the dead. In his area, if someone has died, a team comes and prays over the body for twenty four hours. If they don't come back to life, they release them into the Father's hands. I love Hogan's faith.

- **When you pray, alternate your prayers:** Declare what you feel the Holy Spirit is having you declare. Call the soul of the person, by name, to come back to their bodies. In all things seek the wisdom of the Spirit. **Go for it! Do not fear "Death"! Jesus conquered it!**

Stories:

> "And they went out and preached everywhere, while the Lord
> worked with them and confirmed the message by accompanying
> signs"
> (Mark 16:20)

Sometimes the "Signs and Wonders" happen before we can speak. Other times they confirm what we have said.

Since we will be going from Village To Village (V2V)© then our approach will be different from a typical Gospel Festival style. This will not necessarily be about one person preaching but maybe several of our team taking time to share their testimonies. Sharing about what God has done for you is one of the most powerful sermons there is.

> "We proclaim to you <u>what we ourselves have actually seen
> and heard</u> so that you may have fellowship with us. And our
> fellowship is with the Father and with his Son, Jesus Christ"
> (1 John 1:3 NLT)

Just imagine that you come to a village and there is a person who has pain in their back. What if someone in our team were to tell them of the time that Jesus healed their back pain when someone prayed for them? This person in the village has heard a story of God doing for somebody else what He would like to do for them. Our team member's testimony is important for creating an expectation for God to heal again.

Let us consider another example. When we go to these villages some of the people may never have heard of Jesus, and why He came to earth. This is where we can share the story of how we accepted Jesus as our Lord and Savior. We need to present this Gospel in a way that people will understand. Jesus said that it is the Holy Spirit's role to convict people of sin, not ours (John 16:8), so don't use judgmental words, we are not their judges. Our role is to tell of what the Lord has done for us, because we are witnesses! (Acts 1:8)

Sharing how you came to Christ:

Here are the three steps to sharing your salvation story:

- Give a brief description of your life before you gave your life to Jesus! Were you searching for God? Were you running from God?

- Explain the events around the time that you gave your life to Jesus. Were you searching for answers? Were you feeling a prompting or conviction of needing to make things right with God? Who did God use to introduce you to Jesus? There is no "Sinner's Prayer" in the Bible. However, it is appropriate for someone to pray a prayer that acknowledges this exchange. **Repentance is an issue of the heart first, then the mouth (prayer).**

  Here is an example of an appropriate prayer – **"Jesus, forgive me of the sin of living for myself. I give my life to you. Amen!"** You can also tell them the pray that you prayed when you accepted Jesus. That is totally appropriate. You can lead them in that prayer, if you feel confident. Just remember to keep it simple and not full of Christian jargon. **The unbeliever needs to understand what they are praying.**

- Explain the difference that Jesus has made in your life. If you used to be fearful then how did He help? If you were confused then how did you change? Even if you were rich, happy, and enjoying life, then what is the change now?

Sharing a testimony of healing, provision, or reconciliation:

Here are three steps to sharing a testimony of healing, or financial provision, or God restoring a relationship:

- Give a brief explanation of your life before the illness or need.

- Explain the events surrounding the time of your illness or need. What were you going through?

- Explain how Jesus answered your prayers. If you needed deliverance from a demon then phrase it more like this - "I felt troubled inside. Somebody prayed for me and all the trouble inside stopped" – If you received a physical healing then explain how it happened and how you feel now. The same with a financial need or a broken relationship being restored.

Guidelines to remember:

1. **Do not use too much Bible language, or "Christian" phrases!** The unsaved do not understand the Bible. When Peter visited the Gentiles (Acts 10:1-48), he shared about the vision that he had. Sharing a dream or vision is acceptable because it is like Jesus using parables to explain the Gospel of the Kingdom. **Just make sure the dreams, or visions, are not confusing. Make sure you can give a clear, relevant, meaning to the dream or vision. If not, then don't share it because you'll sound weird and crazy.** Simply talk about what Jesus has done in your life. People will relate, because they are going through the same things that you are. **Jesus makes sense of life for us! So, Be Clear, Be Brief, Be Honest and Be Sincere!**

2. **DO NOT GET INTO ARGUMENTS with people!** If people of different faiths come, LOVE them. SHOW them Jesus by your behavior.

God bless you as you go Village To Village (V2V)©

Printed in Great Britain
by Amazon